THE BOWL OF SAQI

THE BOWL OF SAQI

A Sufi Book of Days

Modern Reader's Edition

Hazrat Pir-o-Murshid
Inayat Khan

Edited and Annotated by
Pir Netanel Miles-Yépez

The Inayati-Maimuni Order
Boulder, Colorado
2021

*"The old shall be renewed,
and the new shall be made holy."*
— Rabbi Avraham Yitzhak Kook

Copyright © 2021 Netanel Miles-Yépez
Third edition. All rights reserved.

This book has been produced for the Inayati-Maimuni Order in cooperation with Albion-Andalus Books.

No part of this book may be reproduced or transmitted in any form or by any means, electronic or mechanical, including photocopy, recording, or any information storage or retrieval system, except for brief passages in connection with a critical review, without permission in writing from the publisher:

Albion-Andalus, Inc.
P. O. Box 19852
Boulder, CO 80308
www.albionandalus.com

Design and composition by Albion-Andalus Books
Cover design by D.A.M. Cool Graphics
Cover image: "Rose Heart and Wings" by Netanel Miles-Yépez.
Mehndi design used from Vecteezy.com

ISBN: 978-1-953220-99-8 (HC)
ISBN: 978-1-953220-03-5 (PB)

Manufactured in the United States of America

Toward the One
The Perfection of Love, Harmony, and Beauty
The Only Being
United with all the Illuminated Souls
Who form the Embodiment of the Message
The Spirit of Guidance

Contents

Editor's Preface	ix
January	1
February	13
March	25
April	37
May	49
June	65
July	77
August	91
September	103
October	115
November	127
December	141
Urs Calendar	153
Index	155
Biography	

Editor's Preface

Despite the similarities of sound and context between the culturally separate homonyms *saqi* and *saki (saké)*, the title of this work is actually *The Bowl of Saqi* and not *A Bowl of Saki*, as some have occasionally read it. Nevertheless, it is an interesting coincidence that the Japanese word for rice-wine fits so neatly into this title, especially as the Persian word of similar pronunciation actually means 'wine-bearer,' or 'one who pours the wine.' In a Sufi context, the *saqi* is the *murshid*, or spiritual 'guide,' who pours the wine of divine love from their own bowl into the bowl of the *murid*, or spiritual aspirant, leading to an intoxication with the divine beloved. But, on another level, the *saqi* is also the Spirit of Guidance itself, as the following poem from the personal notebooks of Hazrat Inayat Khan (1882-1927) makes clear . . .

> Your light which rises in my heart,
> May in the hearts of my murids shine.
> The juice that intoxicated me so,
> O Saqi, give my murids that wine.
> Surround my murids with Your beauty,
> Create in them Your harmony divine,
> Give them sympathy for one another,
> May they forget the world's mine and thine.*

Another meaning implicit in this title has more to do with a Sufi's capacity to receive. A Sufi must always have an empty 'bowl' with which to receive divine love from the beloved. Thus,

---

* Adapted into modern English from the *Complete Works of Pir-o-Murshid Hazrat Inayat Khan, Original Texts: Sayings, Part II.*

The Bowl of Saqi

we must continually go through a process of self-emptying (often referred to in the aphorisms of this collection) in order to become a proper vessel of love. Sometimes it is the pouring out of self-conceit, and sometimes it is simply the sharing of love, the outpouring of love from 'bowl to bowl,' as it were.

The title, *The Bowl of Saqi* (originally *Saki*), was actually chosen by the disciples of Hazrat Inayat Khan (though he had used the phrase in his lectures) when this collection was first published in England in late 1921 or early 1922.* Contained in it were 366 aphorisms which might be used as meditations for the days of the year. These had been selected from the teachings of the master, many coming from his lectures, while others were taken from his personal notebooks.

While the work of Inayat Khan is certainly universalist and egalitarian, he nevertheless spoke, according to the conventions of his day, using the masculine 'he' as inclusive of the feminine 'she,' in an English that might seem somewhat archaic today. For this and many other reasons, I have chosen to re-edit *The Bowl of Saqi* for clarity in modern English, making it gender-inclusive in accord with current values. I have also annotated the aphorisms in places where I thought it necessary to explain non-English vocabulary and to note important days on the calendar of Inayati Sufis.

Despite such edits, I believe *The Bowl of Saqi* may still be read as the words of Inayat Khan, and still represents his intentions. Indeed, it may actually represent his intentions more clearly than the original for the modern reader. Nevertheless, because I have made these adjustments to the language, it must be understood that this edition is necessarily an interpretation of the original, made according to the best of my own understanding and liable to error. Thus, I must take full responsibility for any errors I may

---

* In December 1921, the new book was announced in the quarterly publication *Sufism* with the words: "a collection of some of the most striking and arresting sayings of Pir-o-Murshid, arranged in the form of a daily textbook." *Ibid.*

Editor's Preface

have introduced into it. If those errors are few, it is owing to the proofreading and careful editing suggestions of my student, Daniel Jami.

It is my hope that you will enjoy these aphorisms and use them daily to re-attune to the blessed presence of the beloved.

Netanel Mu'in ad-Din Miles-Yépez
Boulder, Colorado, February 5th, 2021

> "Mysticism
> Without devotion
> Is like uncooked food,
> It can never be assimilated."
> — *The Bowl of Saqi*

JANUARY

January 1

As water in a fountain
Flows as one stream
And falls in many drops,
Divided by time and space,
So too the revelations
Of the one stream of truth.

January 2

All names and forms
Are garments and covers
Under which the one life is hidden.

January 3

Truth without a veil
Is always uninteresting
To the human mind.

January 4

When you stand
With your back to the Sun,
Your shadow is before you;
When you turn to face the Sun,
Your shadow falls behind you.

January 5

No one has seen God and lived;
To see God, we must be non-existent.

January 6

The truth cannot be spoken;
That which can be spoken is not the truth.

January 7

The only power for the mystic
Is the power of love.

January 8

If people actually knew their own religion,
How tolerant they would become,
How free from resentment against
The religion of others.

January 9

The real meaning of crucifixion
Is to crucify the false self
So that the true self might arise.
As long as the false self is not crucified,
The true self is not realized.*

January 10

An ideal is beyond explanation.
To analyze God is to dethrone God.

January 11

Where the flame of love rises,
The knowledge of God unfolds itself.

---

* The Latin *crucifigere* literally means, 'to attach to a cross,' referring to the Roman punishment of nailing persons (most notably, Jesus of Nazareth) to wooden beams.

January 12

Peace is perfected activity;
Perfect is that which is
Complete in all its aspects,
Balanced in each direction,
Under complete control of the will.

January 13

Do not limit God to your virtue;
God is beyond your virtues, pious ones!

January 14

Your inclination
Is the root of the tree
Of your own life.

January 15

Yes, teach your ideas of good,
But do not think to limit God within them.
The goodness of each person
Is unique to that person.

January 16

To learn to adopt the standards of God,
And to cease wishing that the world would
Conform to your own ideas of good
Is the chief lesson of religion.

January 17

Thought
Draws the line of fate.

January 18

Mistaken belief alone misleads;
Single-mindedness leads us to the goal.

January 19

A sovereign is sovereign,
Whether crowned with jewels
Or clad as a beggar.

January 20

To treat everyone as a shrine of God
Is the fulfillment of all religion.

January 21

The wise
Keep the balance
Between love and power,
Keeping the love in their nature
Ever increasing and expanding,
And at the same time,
Strengthening their will
So that the heart
May not easily
Be broken.

January 22

Failure comes
When will surrenders
To reason.

January 23

Success comes when reason,
The storehouse of experience,
Surrenders to will.

January 24

There is an answer to every call;
To those who call on God,
God comes.

January 25

One who thinks
Against their own desire
Is their own enemy.

January 26

The brain speaks through words,
The heart through the eyes' glance,
The soul through a radiance
That charges the atmosphere,
Magnetizing all.

January 27

Love is the merchandise
Which all the world demands;
If you store it in your heart,
Every soul will become
Your customer.

January 28

Sincerity is the jewel that forms
In the shell of the heart.

January 29

Self-pity
Is the worst poverty;
It overwhelms you,
Until you see nothing
But illness, trouble, and pain.

January 30

The heart is not living
Until it has experienced pain.

January 31

The pleasures of life are blinding;
It is love alone that removes rust from the heart,
The mirror of the soul.

FEBRUARY

February 1

The pain of love is the dynamite
That breaks open the heart,
Even if it is as hard as rock.

February 2

Our virtues are made of love,
And our sins are caused by a lack of it.

February 3

Love is the essence of all
Religion, mysticism, and philosophy.

February 4

The fire of devotion
Purifies the heart of the devotee,
And leads to spiritual freedom.

February 5 *

Mysticism
Without devotion
Is like uncooked food,
It can never be assimilated.

February 6

A person who stores evil in their heart
Cannot see beauty.

---

* The *urs* or death anniversary of Hazrat Pir-o-Murshid Inayat Khan. He died at 8:20 A.M., in Delhi, India, 1927. Called *Visalat*, 'return' or 'reconnection,' among Inayati Sufis.

February 7

The wise,
By studying nature,
Enter into unity through variety,
And realize the personality of God
By sacrificing their own.

February 8

Love manifests
Toward those whom we like as love,
Toward those whom we do not like
As forgiveness.

February 9

Love brought us
From the world of unity
To the world of variety,
And the same force
Can take us back
To the world of unity
From the world of variety.

February 10

Whoever knows the mystery of vibrations,
Indeed, knows all things.

February 11

A person who arrives
At the state of indifference
Without experiencing interest in life
Is incomplete and apt to be tempted
By interest at any moment;
A person who arrives
At the state of indifference
By going through interest,
Attains a blessed state.

February 12

Wisdom is greater
And more difficult to attain
Than intellect, piety, or spirituality.

February 13

Wisdom is intelligence in its pure essence,
Which is not necessarily dependent upon
The knowledge of names and forms.

February 14

We form our future by our actions;
Every good or bad action spreads its vibrations
And is known throughout the universe.

February 15

The universe is like a dome;
It vibrates with that which you say in it
And answers the same back to you;
So too is the law of action;
We reap what we sow.

February 16

We are always
Searching for God,
As if far away,
When all the while,
God is nearer
Than our own soul.

February 17

Concentration
And contemplation are great;
But no contemplation is greater
Than the life we have around us everyday.

February 18

The person who expects
To change the world
Will be disappointed.
We must first change our views;
When this is done,
Tolerance will come,
Forgiveness will come,
And there will be nothing
We cannot bear.

February 19

To renounce
What we cannot gain
Is not true renunciation:
It is weakness.

February 20

The religion of the individual
Is the attainment of the soul's desire.
When we are on that path,
We are religious;
When we are off that path,
We are impious.

February 21

The reformer comes
To plough the ground;
The prophet comes
To sow the seed;
The priest comes
To reap the harvest.

February 22

Life is an opportunity
Given to satisfy the hunger
And thirst of the soul.

February 23

Truth alone can succeed;
Lying is a waste of time
And a loss of energy.

February 24

Do not fear God,
But consciously regard
God's pleasure and displeasure.

February 25

Failing ourselves, we fail all;
Conquering the self, we win all.

February 26

As we rise above passion,
We begin to know love.

February 27

Believe in God
With childlike faith;
Simplicity with intelligence
Is the sign of the holy ones.

February 28

A person who can
Live up to their own ideal
Is sovereign in life;
A person who cannot
Is life's slave.

February 29

Every moment of life
Is an invaluable opportunity.

MARCH

MARCH 1

Nature speaks louder
Than the call from the minaret.*

MARCH 2

The priest gives a benediction
From the Church;
The bowing branches of a tree
Give a blessing from God.

---

* A minaret is a structure of Islamic architecture, usually a tower from which the Islamic call to prayer *(azan)* is given by the *muezzin*.

March 3

The soul brings its light from heaven;
The mind acquires its knowledge from earth.
Therefore, even when the soul believes,
The mind can still doubt.

March 4

Those who throw sand at the Sun,
Will have sand fall in their eyes.

March 5

We create
Our own disharmony.

March 6

The real abode of God
Is in the human heart;
When it is frozen with bitterness or hatred,
The doors of the shrine are closed,
Its light hidden.

March 7

It is a false love
That does not yield the claim of 'I';
The first and last lesson of love is
'I am not.'

March 8

You cannot be both horse and rider
At the same time.

March 9

It is more important
To know the truth about one's self
Than to try to find out the truth
Of heaven and hell.

March 10

Everyone's pursuit
Is according to their own evolution.

March 11

One sees what one sees;
Beyond it, one cannot see.

March 12

The source of truth
Is within the human being;
The human being is
the object of its realization.

March 13

As life unfolds itself to us,
The first lesson we learn is humility.

March 14

God is Truth,
And Truth is God.

March 15

Until we lose ourselves in the vision of God,
We cannot be said to live truly.

March 16

At every step of our evolution,
The realization of God changes.

March 17

Truly, one is victorious
Who has conquered the self.

March 18

Prayer is the greatest virtue,
The only way of being free from all sin.

March 19

It is the sincere devotee
Who knows best
How to humble the self
Before God.

March 20

It is wise to see all things,
And yet turn our eyes
From all that should be overlooked.

March 21

Our soul is blessed
With the impression of God's glory
Whenever our lips praise God.

March 22

There is one teacher, God alone;
We are all God's students.

March 23

All earthly knowledge
Is a cloud covering the Sun.

March 24

The first sign
Of the realization of Truth
Is tolerance.

March 25

One who is filled
With knowledge
Of names and forms
Has no room for
The knowledge of God.

March 26

We are closer to God
Than fish to the ocean.

March 27

We start our lives
Trying to be teachers;
It is harder to learn to be a student.

March 28

Until the heart is empty,
It cannot receive the knowledge of God.

March 29

According to our evolution,
We know Truth.

March 30

We can never humble
Our limited self sufficiently
Before limitless perfection.

March

March 31

Even to utter the name of God
Is a blessing that can fill the soul
With light and joy and happiness
As nothing else can do.

APRIL

April 1

When we praise
The beauty of God,
Our souls are filled with bliss.

April 2

Sympathy is the root of religion;
As long as the spirit of sympathy
Is living in your heart,
You have the light of religion.

April 3

Life is a misery for one
Who is absorbed only in the self.

April 4

To give sympathy is sovereignty;
To desire it from others is captivity.

April 5

God speaks to the ear of every heart,
But not every heart hears God.

April 6

As we can see when our eyes are open,
So we can understand when our hearts are open.

April 7

Being transparent to the self
Is the recognition of God.

April 8

As the light of the Sun
Helps the plant to grow,
The divine spirit helps the soul
Toward its perfection.

April 9

Things are worthwhile when we seek them;
Only then do we know their value.

April 10

When we look at the ocean,
We can only see the part of it that
Comes within our range of vision;
So it is with the Truth.

April 11

It does not matter
In what way a person
Offers respect and reverence
To the God they worship;
It only matters how sincere
They are in their offering.

April 12

The ideal of God is a bridge
Connecting the limited life with the unlimited;
Whoever travels over this bridge
Passes safely from the limited life
To the life unlimited.

April 13

One who wants to understand
Will understand.

April 14

We are the picture
Reflected in our imagination;
We are as large or as small
As we think ourselves.

April 15

The great teachers of humanity
Become streams of love.

April 16

"God is love"— *
Three words which
Open an unending realm
For the thinker who
Desires to probe the depths
Of life's secret.

April 17

It is the surface of the sea
That makes waves and roaring breakers;
The depths are silent.

---

* The New Testament, 1 John 4:8, 16.

April 18

Our success or failure
Depends upon the
Harmony or disharmony
Of our individual will
With the divine will.

April 19

The wave realizes, "I am the sea,"
And by falling into the sea,
Prostrates to its God.

April 20

The secret of happiness
Is hidden under the cover
Of spiritual knowledge.

April 21

The soul is first born
Into the false self,
And is blind;
Through the true self,
The soul opens its eyes.

April 22

To learn the lesson of how to live
Is more important than
Psychic or occult knowledge.

April 23

Knowledge without love
Is lifeless.

April 24

The aim of the mystic
Is to remain close to the idea of unity
And to discover how we are united.

April 25

Sleep is comfortable,
But waking is interesting.

April 26

Every moment
Has its special message.

April 27

To make God a reality
Is the real object of worship.

April 28

Every passion, every emotion
Has its effect upon the mind;
Every change of mind, however slight,
Has its effect upon the body.

April 29

When souls meet one another,
What truth they can exchange!
It is uttered in silence,
Yet always reaches its goal.

April

April 30

All gains,
Material, spiritual,
Moral, or mystical,
Are in answer
To our character.

MAY

May 1

You can have
All good things—
Wealth, friends, kindness,
Love to give and receive—
Once you have learned
Not to be blinded by them,
Learned to escape disappointment
And repugnance at the idea
That things are not
As you want them to be.

May 2

The truth
Need not be veiled,
For it veils itself
From the eyes of the ignorant.

May 3

No one should
Allow their mind
To be a vehicle
For others to use;
Those who do not
Direct their own minds
Lack mastery.

May 4

Rest of mind
Is as necessary
As rest of body,
And yet we always
Keep the former in motion.

May 5

Those who have given
Deep thought to the world
Are those who have
Controlled the activity
Of their minds.

May 6

Unity in realization
Is far greater than
Unity in variety.

May 7

The afterlife
Is like a gramophone
To which our minds bring records.
If they are harsh,
The instrument produces harsh notes;
If beautiful, then it will sing beautiful songs.
It will play the same records
You have experienced
In this life.

May 8

The person who depends
Upon the eyes for sight,
The ears for hearing,
And the mouth for speech,
Is still dead.

May

May 9

We cover our spirit
Under our body,
Our light under a bushel; *
We never allow the spirit
To become conscious of itself.

May 10

When we
Devote ourselves
To the thought of God,
All illumination and revelation is ours.

---

* Reference to The New Testament, Matthew 5:15.

May 11

God-communication
Is the best communication
That true spiritualism can teach us. *

May 12

The mystic desires what
Omar Khayyám calls "wine"— **
The wine of Christ ***
Which once tasted
Eliminates all thirst.

---

* In Inayat Khan's time, there was much fascination with the occult and psychic phenomena, especially communication with disembodied spirits, often called "spiritualism."
** Wine in this context is the intoxicating love of God. Omar Khayyám (1048–1131) was a Persian poet, author of the *Rubaiyat* (quatrains).
*** The "wine of Christ" is a reference to the wine of the Last Supper, a symbol of the blood of Christ, Christ's salvific compassion or love.

May 13

Our limited self
Is a wall separating us
From the self of God.

May 14

The wisdom
And justice of God
Are within us,
And yet, far away,
Hidden by the veil
Of the limited self.

May 15

One who
Looks for a reward
Is smaller than the reward;
One who yields it
Has risen above it.

May 16

The poverty of one
Who gives is a treasure
When compared with
The riches of one
Who does not.

May 17

Love for God
Is the expansion of the heart,
And all actions that come
From the lover of God are virtues;
They cannot be otherwise.

May 18

God is the ideal
That raises humanity
To the utmost of perfection.

May 19

The wise treat
Acquaintances like friends;
The foolish treat
Friends like acquaintances;
The lost treat
Friends and acquaintances like strangers—
You cannot help that person.

May 20

Insight into life
Is the real religion;
That alone can help us understand.

May 21

The realization that
The whole of life must be 'give and take'
Is the realization of spiritual truth
And true democracy;
Until this spirit is formed in the individual,
The world cannot be elevated.

May 22

The perfection of life
Is found in following our own ideal,
Not in judging the ideals of others—
Leave others to follow their own ideal.

May 23

Everyone's desire is in accord
With their own evolution;
That for which they are ready
Is desirable for them.

May 24

Discussion is for
Those who say,
"What I say is right;
What you say is wrong."
A sage is silent on the matter;
Hence, there is no discussion.

May 25

Tolerance does not come
By learning, but by insight,
By understanding that each person
Should be allowed to travel along the path
Which is most suited to their temperament.

May 26

So long as we have a longing
To obtain any particular object,
We cannot go further than that object.

May 27

One's paths is one's own;
Let others accomplish their own desires,
So that they may be able to rise above them
To the eternal goal.

May 28

To control the self
Is to control everything.

May 29

"God is love." *
When love is awakened in the heart,
God is awakened there, too.

---

* The New Testament, 1 John 4:8, 16.

May 30

All the disharmony
Caused by religious differences
Is the result of our failure to understand
That religion is one, Truth is one, God is one.
How can there be two religions?

May 31

Using friendship
For selfish motives
Is like mixing bitter poison
With a sweet rose-petal syrup.

JUNE

June 1

Our bodily appetites
Lead us away from our heart's desire;
Our heart's desire leads us away
From the abode of the soul.

June 2

Words are but shadows
Of thoughts and feelings.

June 3

The more elevated the soul,
The broader its view.

June 4

A friend's secret
Should be kept as one's own;
A friend's faults
Should be hidden as one's own.

June 5

Forbearance, patience, and tolerance
Are the only conditions that keep
Two individual hearts united.

June 6

We blame others
For our sorrows and misfortunes,
Not perceiving that we
Create our world.

June 7

Nobody appears inferior to us
When our hearts are kindled with kindness
And our eyes are open to the vision of God.

June 8

Selfishness
Keeps one blind in life.

June 9

For every soul,
The final victory
In the battle of life
Is to rise above that
Which once we valued most.

June 10

When power leads and wisdom follows,
The face of wisdom is veiled and falls;
When wisdom leads and power follows,
They arrive safely at their destination.

June 11

Our conduct in life
Depends on what we hold in our thoughts.

June 12

A person who can be detached enough
To witness and attempt to help all those
Whom circumstances have placed about them,
Becomes enriched, inheriting the sovereignty of God.

June 13

True justice cannot be perceived
Until the veil of selfishness
Is removed from the eyes.

June 14

Our thoughts determine
The happiness or unhappiness we experience.

June 15

Love is the best means
Of making the heart capable
Of reflecting the soul's power;
Love in the sense of pain
Rather than pleasure;
Every blow opens a door
From whence the soul's power
Emerges.

June 16

Every experience
Of the physical, astral, or mental plane
Is just a dream before the soul.

June 17

The fire of devotion
Purifies the heart of the devotee
And leads to spiritual freedom.

June 18

When love's fire
Produces its flame,
It illuminates
The devotee's path
Like a torch,
And darkness vanishes.

June 19

It is mistrust that misleads;
Sincerity leads us straight to the goal.

June 20

Love lies in service;
Only that which is not done
For name or fame,
Nor for the appreciation or thanks
Of those for whom it is done,
Is love's service.

June 21

The soul is light;
Darkness is caused
By the deadness of the heart;
Pain makes it alive.

June 22

The quality of forgiveness
That burns everything except beauty
Is the quality of love.

June 23

Each of us composes
The music of our own life;
If we injure another,
We break the harmony
And there is discord
In the melody
Of our life.

June 24

One who sincerely
Seeks a real purpose in life
Is also sought by that purpose.

June 25

Through motion and change,
This life becomes intelligible.
We live a life of change,
But it is constancy we seek;
It is this innate desire of the soul
That leads the human being to God.

June 26

Every one of us
Has a definite vocation,
And our vocation is the light
That illuminates our life.
Those who disregard
Their own vocation
Are as lamps
Unlit.

June 27

The heart sleeps
Until awakened to life by a blow.
As with a rock, the hidden fire flashes
When struck by another rock.

June 28

The awakened heart says,
"I must give; I must not demand."
Thus it enters into a state that
Leads to a constant happiness.

June 29

The worlds are held together
By the heat of the Sun.
We are like atoms
Held in position by
The eternal Sun we call God.
Within us is the same
Central power we call
The light or love of God;
With it we hold together
The human beings
Within our sphere;
Lacking it,
We let them fall.

June 30

When we dive within,
We find that the real self is above
The perpetual motion of the universe.

JULY

July 1

Our pride and satisfaction
In what we know
Limits the scope of our vision.

July 2

If we desire peace in the world,
We must first create peace in ourselves;
Lacking peace within,
No amount of effort
Can bring about
The desired result.

July 3

Knowledge of self
Is the essential knowledge;
It gives us an understanding of humanity.
In the understanding of the human being
Lies the understanding of nature
That reveals the law of creation.

July 4

While some blame others
For causing them harm,
The wise take themselves to task.

July 5 *

Whatever their faith,
The wise have always
Been able to meet one another
Beyond those boundaries
Of external form and convention,
Which, though natural
And necessary to human life,
Separate humanity.

July 6

It is the Message
That proves the messenger,
Not the claim.

---

* The birthday of Hazrat Pir-o-Murshid Inayat Khan, 11:35 P.M., Baroda (Vadodara), Gujarat, India, 1882. Called *Viladat* (birthday) among Inayati Sufis.

July 7

Every soul
Has a definite task;
Only the fulfillment of
Your individual purpose
Can lead you aright.
Illumination comes to one
Through the medium
Of their talent.

July 8

Some only judge from
Their own moral standpoint;
The wise also see
From the point-of-view
Of others.

July 9

While some rejoice over their own rise,
And sorrow over their own fall,
The wise take both as
Natural consequences of life.

July 10

It is the lover of God,
Whose heart is filled with devotion,
Who can commune with God,
Not those who seek to analyze God
With the intellect.

July 11

Do not bemoan the past
Or worry about the future;
Try to make the best of today.

July 12

Those who quicken
The feelings of others
With joy or gratitude
Add to their own lives.

July 13

Praise cannot exist without blame;
It has no existence without its opposite.

July 14

Riches and power may vanish
Because they are outside ourselves;
Only that which is within can we call our own.

July 15

The world is evolving
From imperfection toward perfection;
It needs all our love and sympathy;
Great tenderness and vigilance
Is required from each of us.

July 16

The heart of every person,
Whether good or bad,
Is the abode of God,
And care should be taken
Never to wound anyone
By word or deed.

July 17

We should take care
To remove from ourselves
Any thorns
That prick us
Through the personalities
Of others.

July 18

There is a light
Within every soul;
It only needs the clouds
That overshadow it to break
For it to shine.

July 19

The soul's true happiness
Lies in experiencing inward joy,
And will never be fully satisfied
With external pleasures.
Its connection is with God,
And nothing short of perfection
Will ever satisfy it.

July 20

Life's blows
Pierce the heart
And awaken feelings
To sympathize with others;
While comfort lulls us to sleep
And we lose awareness of all.

July 21

The greatest religion
Is the study of life;
There is no greater
Or more interesting
Subject.

July 22

We can learn virtue
From the greatest sinners
If we consider them our teachers.

July 23

Warmth melts and cold freezes;
Ice melting in a warm place
Spreads and covers that place,
Whereas a drop of water in a cold place
Freezes and becomes limited.
Repentance has the effect
Of melting and spreading
What was frozen in its warmth,
Causing the heart to expand
And become universal;
While hardening of the heart
Brings limitation.

July 24

There should be
A balance to all our actions;
To be either extreme or lukewarm
Is equally bad.

July 25

Spirit
Is the real part of us;
The body is only its garment.
As one cannot find peace
At the tailor's shop
Merely because their coat
Comes from there,
Neither can the spirit
Obtain true happiness
From the earth
Just because its body
Belongs to it.

July 26

Every purpose
Has a birth and a death;
Therefore, God is beyond purpose.

July 27

Belief and disbelief
Divide humanity into sects,
Blinding our eyes
To the vision
Of the oneness
Of all life.

July 28

Spirit can only love spirit;
In loving form, it deludes itself.

July 29

To love is one thing,
To understand is another.
One who loves is a devotee;
One who understands is a friend.

July 30

Among a million
Believers in God
There is scarcely one
Who makes God a reality.

July 31

The soul feels suffocated
When the doors of the heart
Are closed.

AUGUST

August 1

Understanding
Makes the troubles of life
Lighter to bear.

August 2

The same herb
Planted in different
Atmospheric conditions
Will vary in form accordingly,
But will retain its characteristics.

August 3

Before envying
Someone else's position,
Think by what difficulty
They arrived at it.

August 4

Life is what it is;
You cannot change it,
But you can always
Change yourself.

August 5

Life is a continual
Series of experiences,
One leading to another
Until the soul arrives
At its destination.

August 6

External life
Is the shadow
Of an inner reality.

August 7

At the cost of one failure,
The wise learn a lesson
For their whole life.

August 8

The more you evolve spiritually,
The less you are understood
By others.

August 9

One word
Can be more precious
Than all the treasures of the earth.

August 10

Narrowness is primitive;
It is breadth of heart
That proves one's evolution.

August 11

It is simpler
To find a way to heaven
Than to find a way on earth.

August 12

It is God who
By our hands
Designs and executes
God's intended plans
In nature.

August 13

The lover of nature
Is the true worshipper of God.

August 14

In the country,
You see the glory of God;
In the city, you glorify God's name.

August 15

The pain of life
Is the price paid
For the quickening of the heart.

August 16

Words that enlighten the soul
Are more precious than jewels.

August 17

Love is the current coin
Of all peoples in all periods.

August 18

Do not take the example of another
As an excuse for your own wrongdoing.

August 19

Overlook the faults of others;
but do not partake of them,
even in the smallest degree.

August 20

Cleverness and complexity
Are not necessarily wisdom.

August 21

The entire world's treasure
Is too small a price to pay
For a word that kindles the soul.

August 22

One whose sympathy is awake
Is living;
One whose heart is asleep
Is dead.

August 23

By our thoughts,
We prepare the happiness or unhappiness
We experience.

August 24

Put your trust in God for support,
And see God's hidden hand
Working through all things.

August 25

Faith is the ABC
Of the realization of God;
This faith begins by prayer.

August 26

Passion is the smoke
Of love's fire,
Emotion its glow,
And unselfishness its flame
That illuminates the path.

August 27

The soul of Christ [*]
Is the light of the universe.

---

[*] Christ, the 'anointed one,' or Messiah.

August 28

Death is a tax
The soul has to pay
For having acquired
A name and form.

August 29

A pure life
And a clean conscience
Are as two wings
Attached to the soul.

August 30

The giver is
Greater than the gift.

August

August 31

One who has spent
Has used;
One who has collected
Has lost;
But one who has given,
Has saved the treasure
Forever.

SEPTEMBER

September 1

Joy and sorrow
Are for each other:
If it were not for joy,
There would be no sorrow;
If it were not for sorrow,
There would be no joy
To experience.

September 2

Self-pity is the cause
Of all of life's grievances.

September 3

How can the unlimited be limited?
All that seems limited
Is beyond limitation
In its depth.

September 4

Pleasure blocks inspiration;
Pain clears its way.

September 5

There is no source of happiness
Other than that found
In the heart of humanity.

September 6

Happy is the person
Who does good for others;
Miserable is the person
Who expects good from others.

September 7

One virtue is more powerful
Than a thousand vices.

September 8

The soul is either raised or cast down
By the power of its own
Thoughts, words, or deeds.

September 9

Love is the divine mother's arms;
When those arms are spread,
Every soul falls into them.

September 10

It is the fruit
That makes the tree bow.

September 11

In order to learn forgiveness,
One must first learn tolerance.

September 12

The first step
Toward forgiveness
Is forgetting.

September 13 *

The only way to live
In the midst of inharmonious influences
Is to strengthen the willpower
And endure all things,
Keeping fineness of character
And nobility of manner
Together with an ever-living
Heart full of love.

---

* On September 13th, 1910, Hazrat Pir-o-Murshid Inayat Khan departed from India to come to the West at the direction of his *murshid*. This is known as *Hejirat* among Inayati Sufis.

September 14

Devotion to a spiritual teacher
Is not for the sake of the teacher;
It is for God's sake.

September 15

To become cold
From the coldness of the world
Is weakness.
To become broken
By the hardness of the world
Is feebleness.
But to live in the world,
And rise above it,
Is like walking on water.

September 16

God alone
Deserves all love;
The freedom of love
Is in giving it to God.

September 17

Love has the power
To open the door of eternal life.

September 18

Love has its limitations
When directed toward limited beings;
But love directed to God has no limitations.

September 19

No teacher, however great,
can give their knowledge to a student;
The student must create their own knowledge.

September 20

One thing is true:
Although the teacher
Cannot give one knowledge,
The teacher can kindle the light
If there is oil in the lamp.

September 21

Willpower
Is the keynote of mastery,
And asceticism
Is the development
Of willpower.

September 22

Real generosity
Is an unfailing sign
Of spirituality.

September 23

There are two kinds of generosity,
The real and its shadow;
The former is prompted by love,
The latter by vanity.

September 24

It is better to pay
Than to receive from the vain,
For such favors demand
Ten times their worth.

September 25

The sovereignty of heaven
Is in the hearts of those
Who realize God.

September 26

In order to relieve
The hunger of others,
We must forget our own.

September 27

It is when we lose
The idea of separateness
And feel unified with all creation
That our eyes are opened
And we see the cause of all things.

September

September 28

To fall beneath your ideal
Is to lose a share of your life.

September 29

The wise of all ages have taught us
That knowing the divine being
Is the only true life and reality.

September 30

As the Ganges* purifies all
Who plunge into its sacred waters,
When the stream of love flows with full strength,
It purifies all that stands in its way.

---

* The Ganges, or Ganga, is a river in India considered a manifestation of the goddess in the Hindu tradition.

OCTOBER

October 1

A soul's attainment
Is in accord with its evolution.

October 2

When God's call comes,
It always means that you must sacrifice
Something very dear to you.

October 3

Renunciation
Is always for a purpose:
It is to kindle the soul
So that nothing
May hold it back
From God.
When it is kindled,
The life of renunciation
Is unnecessary.

October 4

There are those who,
Like a lighted candle,
Can light other candles.
But the other candles
Must be of wax;
If they are of steel,
They will not burn.

October 5

There is no greater scripture than nature,
For nature is life itself.

October 6

Wisdom is only learned gradually;
Not every soul is ready
To receive or understand
The complexity of life's purpose.

October 7

It is a high level on love's ladder
When one really learns to love another
With a love that asks nothing in return.

October 8

Love alone
Is the fountain
From which all virtues fall
As drops of sparkling water.

October 9

The whole purpose of life
Is to make God a reality.

October 10

If you seek
The good in every soul,
You will always find it:
God is in all things;
God is in all beings.

October 11

The knowledge of God
Is beyond human reason.
The secret of God
Is hidden in the knowledge of unity.

October 12

Seek God in all souls,
Good and bad, wise and foolish,
Attractive and unattractive;
In the depths of each is God.

October 13

When there is disharmony in ourselves,
How can we spread harmony?

October 14

Our innermost being
Is the real being of God.

October 15

Love itself
Is the healing power
And the remedy for all pain.

October 16

By loving, forgiving, and serving,
It is possible for your whole life to become
A vision of God's sublime beauty.

October 17

Mysticism,
To the mystic,
Is both science and religion.

October 18

The principles of mysticism
Rise from the heart of the human being;
They are learned by intuition
And proven by reason.

October 19

Your work in life
Must be your religion,
Whatever your occupation be.

October 20

The true joy of every soul
Is in realizing the divine spirit;
The absence of realization
Keeps the soul in despair.

October 21

Beyond
The narrow boundaries
Of race and creed,
We can all unite,
Because we all belong
To one God.

October 22

All forms of worship or prayer
Draw one closer to God.

October 23

When one is separated from God in thought,
Belief is of no use, and worship of little use.

October 24

The source of the realization of truth is within;
The self is the object of realization.

October 25

True self-denial
Is losing one's self in God.

October 26

It is more important
To discover the truth about one's self
Than to discover the truth of heaven and hell.

October 27

According to our evolution,
We know Truth;
And the more we know,
The more we find there is to know.

OCTOBER 28

A person who is
Filled with the knowledge
Of names and forms
Has no capacity
For the knowledge
Of Truth.

OCTOBER 29

We make a mistake
When we begin
To cultivate the heart
By wanting
To sow the seed ourselves,
Instead of leaving the sowing
To God.

October 30

We start our lives teaching,
So it is very hard for us
To learn to become students.
There are many
Whose only difficulty in life
Is that they are already teaching;
What we have to learn is discipleship.
There is only one teacher,
God.

October 31

Earthly knowledge
Is like the clouds dimming one's sight;
It is the breaking of these clouds,
In other words 'purity of heart,'
That builds capacity
And allows the knowledge of God
To rise.

NOVEMBER

November 1

The self stands as a wall
Between us and God.

November 2

It is a patient pursuit
To bring water from the depths of the earth;
You have to dig through a lot of mud
Before you reach the water of life.

November 3

In our search for truth,
The first and last lesson is love.
There must be no separation,
No 'I am' and 'you are not.'
Until we have arrived
At that selfless consciousness,
We cannot know life and truth.

November 4

By the power of prayer,
We open the door of the heart,
In which God, the ever-forgiving,
The all-merciful, abides.

November 5

To be truly sorry for one's errors
Is like opening the doors of heaven.

November 6

Our soul is blessed
With the impression
Of the glory of God
Whenever we praise God.

November 7

As a child learning to walk
Falls a thousand times before it can stand,
And falls again and again,
Until at last it can walk,
So do we as little children
Before God.

November 8

Self-denial is not
Renouncing things,
It is denying the self.
The first lesson of self-denial
Is humility.

November 9

The more elevated the soul,
The broader the outlook.

November 10

Mastery lies not
In merely stilling the mind,
But in directing it toward
Whatever point you desire.

November 11

Our thoughts determine
The happiness or unhappiness we experience.

November 12

When the mind and body are restless,
Nothing in life can be accomplished.
Success is the result of control.

November 13

When speech is controlled, the eyes speak;
The glance says what words can never say.

November 14

Words are but the shells
Of thoughts and feelings.

November 15

Wisdom is not in words;
It is in understanding.

November 16

The message of God
Is like a spring of water—
It rises and falls
And makes its way by itself.

November 17

If the eyes and ears are open,
The leaves of trees
Become like pages
Of the Bible. *

---

* The third of the "Ten Remembrances" of Inayati Sufis says: "There is one holy writing, the sacred book of nature, the only scripture that truly enlightens its reader."

November 18

The soul of all is one soul,
And the truth is one truth,
Under whatever religion it is hidden.

November 19

Narrowness
Is not necessarily devotion,
Though it often appears to be.

November 20

It is the soul's light
That appears as natural intelligence.

November 21

The wave is the sea itself.
When it rises
In the form of a wave,
It is a wave;
And yet when you look
At the whole,
It is the sea.

November 22

It is not solid wood
That becomes a flute,
It is the empty reed. *

---

* The *ney*, a reed pipe is a traditional instrument of Sufi music.

November 23

Reason is learned
From the ever-changing world;
But true knowledge
Comes from the essence of life.

November 24

God is within you.
You are God's instrument,
And through you,
God expresses the divine self
To the external world.

NOVEMBER 25

Our prayer reaches God
According to the extent
Of our consciousness
In prayer.

NOVEMBER 26

The heart must be empty
In order to receive
The knowledge of God.

NOVEMBER 27

As long as there is
'You' and 'me' in love,
Love is not fully kindled.

November 28

Once you have yielded
Your limited self
To the unlimited, willingly,
You will rejoice so much
In that consciousness
That you will not care
To be small again.

November 29

The deeper your prayers echo
In your own consciousness,
The more audible they are to God.

November

November 30

It is depth of thought
That is powerful,
And sincerity of feeling
That creates atmosphere.

DECEMBER

December 1

The higher you rise,
The wider the margin
Of your view.

December 2

Justice can never be developed
While we are judging others;
Justice is only developed by
Constantly evaluating ourselves.

December 3

Joy and sorrow
Are the light and shadow of life;
Without light and shadow,
No picture is clear.

December 4

The wise submit
To conditions when helpless,
Bowing to the will of God,
But root out the sin that is avoidable
Without sparing a single moment or effort.

December 5

Enviable is one who loves
And asks no return.

December 6

Denying the mutability of life
Is like fancying a motionless sea
That can only exist in one's imagination.

December 7

Learn to live a true life,
And you will know the truth.

December 8

Wisdom is attained
In solitude.

December 9

The seeming death of the body
Is the real birth of the soul.

December 10

As the rose blooms amidst thorns,
So great souls shine through all opposition.

December 11

When the artist
Loses the self in art,
Then the art comes to life.

December 12

Do not do anything with fear,
And fear not what you do.

December 13

Love develops into harmony,
And of harmony is born beauty.

December 14

Those who keep no secrets
Have no depth in their hearts.

December 15

Behind us all
Is one spirit and one life;
How then can we be happy
If our neighbor is not happy?

December 16

The sea of life is in constant motion;
No one can stop its ever-moving waves.
The masterful walk over the waves,
The wise swim in the water,
But the ignorant drown
In the effort to cross.

December 17

The human being's greatest privilege
Is to become a suitable instrument of God.

December 18

The trees of the forest
Silently await God's blessing.

December 19

The plain truth is too simple
For seekers of complexity,
Who always look for things
They cannot understand.

December 20

An unsuccessful person
Often keeps success at bay
Through the impression
Of their former failures.

December 21

The human being
Is a tree of desire;
The roots of that tree
Are in the heart.

December 22

With goodwill
And trust in God,
Self-confidence
And a hopeful
Attitude toward life,
One can always win the battle,
However difficult.

December 23

There are many paths,
And everyone considers
Their own the best and wisest.
Let everyone choose that which
Belongs to their own temperament.

December 24

Failure, either in health or one's affairs,
Means there has been a lack of self-control.

December 25

Love is as the water of the Ganges; *
It is in itself a purification.

December 26

Love is unlimited,
But it needs scope
To expand and rise;
Without that scope,
Life is unhappy.

---

* The Ganges, or Ganga, is a river in India considered a manifestation of the goddess in the Hindu tradition.

December 27

Every wave of the sea, as it rises,
Seems to be stretching its hands upward,
As if to say, "Take me higher!"

December 28

True pleasure lies in
Sharing joy with another.

December 29

A momentary
Gain or loss is not real;
If we knew reality,
We should never grieve
Over the loss of anything
That experience shows
To be only transitory.

December 30

A soul is as great
As the circle of its influence.

December 31

Happiness lies in thinking or doing
That which one considers beautiful.

URS *

15 January – *Ḥaẓrāt Pir-o-Murshid* Samuel (Sūfī Aḥmad Murad) Lewis (d. 1971)

5 February – *Ḥaẓrāt Pir-o-Murshid* (Sūfī) 'Inayat Khan (d. 1927)

28 February – *Ḥaẓrāt Murshid* Earl (Fatha) Engle (d. 1953)

2 March – *Ḥaẓrāta Murshida* Emily Maud (Sophia) Saintsbury-Green (d. 1939)

8 March – *Ḥaẓrāta Murshida* Lucy Marian (Sharifa) Goodenough (d. 1937)

17 June – *Ḥaẓrāt Pir-o-Murshid* Vilāyat Ināyat Khān (d. 2004)

3 July – *Ḥaẓrāt Pir-o-Murshid* Maheboob Khan (d. 1948)

---

* An incomplete list of *urs* (death anniversary) dates of founders and early leaders of Inayati Sufism.

The Bowl of Saqi

3 July – Ḥaẓrat Pir-o-Murshid Zalman (Sulaymān) Schachter-Shalomi (d. 2014)

July 25 – Ḥaẓrat Pir-o-Murshid Richard (Sufi Shirdil Amin) Macko (d. 1991)

30 August – Ḥaẓrata Pirnī-o-Murshida Ada (Rabia) (née Ginsberg) Martin (d. 1947)

26 September – Ḥaẓrat Pir-o-Murshid Fazal Inayat-Khan (d. 1990)

7 October – Ḥaẓrat Shaykh al-Mashā'ikh Sayyid Abū Hāshim Madanī (d. 1907)

30 November – Ḥaẓrat Pir-o-Murshid Musharaff Moulamia Raḥmat Khan (d. 1967)

27 December – Ḥaẓrata Murshida Petronella Fazal Mai Egeling-Grol (d. 1939)

Index

action, 18, 57, 87
art, 145
asceticism, 110
astral plane, 70
atmosphere, 10. 91, 139
beauty, ix, 14, 37, 72, 120, 145
beggar, 77
belief, 7, 89, 123
beloved, ix, xi
Bible, 133
birth, 88, 144
bitterness, 27, 63
blame, 66, 78, 82
blindness, 11, 44, 49, 67, 89
body, 46, 50, 53, 88, 132, 144
bowl, ix, x
brain, 10
bridges, 41
candle, 116
character, 47, 107
children, 23, 130
Christ, 54, 99
Church, 25
cleverness, 97
clouds, 32, 84, 126

coat, 88
coin, 96
concentration, 19
confidence, 149
conscience, 100
contemplation, 19
creation, 78, 112
creed, 122
crucifixion, 4
death, 14, 88, 100, 144, 153
democracy, 59
desire, 9, 21, 38, 42, 54, 60, 62, 65, 73, 77, 131, 148
despair, 122
devotion, 14, 31, 53, 70, 81, 89, 108, 134
discipleship, 126
disharmony, 26, 43, 63, 119
dream, 70
ears, 38, 52, 133
earth, 26, 32, 88, 93, 94, 126, 127
emotion, 46, 99
enemy, 9
eyes, 10, 26, 31, 38, 44, 49, 52, 67, 68, 69, 89, 112, 132, 133
evil, 14
evolution, 28, 30, 34, 60, 94, 115, 124
failure, 8, 23, 43, 63, 93, 148, 150
faith, 23, 79, 99
false self, 4, 44
fame, 71
fate, 6

INDEX

fear, 22, 145

feelings, 65, 82, 85, 90, 112, 132, 139

fire, 14, 70, 74, 99

fish, 33

flute, 135

food, 14

foolish, 58, 119

forbearance, 66

forests, 147

forgiveness, 15, 20, 72, 106, 107, 120, 128

form, 1, 18, 33, 79. 89, 91, 100, 123, 125, 135

fountain, 1, 118

freedom, 14, 70, 109

friendship, 49, 58, 63, 66, 89

fruit, 106

future, 18, 81

Ganges, 113, 150

garment, 1, 88

generosity, 111

gift, 100

good, 6, 18, 49, 83, 105, 118, 119, 149

gramophone, 52

happiness, 35, 43, 69, 74, 85, 88, 98, 104, 105, 131, 146, 150, 152

harmony, ix, 43, 72, 119, 145

hate, 27

healing, 120, 150

hearing, 38, 52

heart, ix, 8, 10, 11, 13, 14, 27, 34, 37, 38, 57, 62, 65, 66, 67, 69,

70, 71, 74, 81, 83, 85, 87, 90, 94, 95, 98, 104, 107, 112, 121, 125, 126, 128, 137, 146, 148

heaven, 26, 28, 94, 112, 124, 129

hell, 28, 124

herb, 91

horses, 27

human beings, 2, 27, 29, 73, 75, 78, 79, 119, 121, 147, 148

humanity, 42, 57, 78, 79, 89, 104

humility, 29, 31, 34, 130

hunger, 22, 112

ideal, 4, 24, 41, 57, 59, 113

illness, 11

illumination, 53, 70, 73, 80, 99

imagination, 41, 143

indifference, 17

inspiration, 104

intellect, 17, 81

intelligence, 18, 23, 134

intoxication, ix, 54

intuition, 121

Jesus, 4

jewels, 7, 10, 96

joy, 35, 82, 85, 103, 122, 142, 151

judgment, 59, 80, 141

juice, ix

justice, 55, 69, 141

lamp, 73, 110

light, ix, 26, 27, 35, 37, 39, 53, 71, 73, 75, 84, 99, 110, 116, 134, 142

Index

lips, 31

love, ix, x, 3, 4, 8, 10, 11, 13, 15, 16, 23, 27, 42, 44, 49, 54, 57, 62, 69, 70, 71, 72, 75, 81, 83, 89, 95, 96, 99, 106, 107, 109, 111, 113, 117, 118, 120, 128, 137, 143, 145, 150

mastery, 50, 110, 131, 146

mental plane, 70

message, 45, 79, 133

messenger, 79

mind, 2, 26, 46, 50, 51, 52, 131, 132

minaret, 25

mirror, 11

moral, 47, 80

mother, 106

mouth, 52

murīd, ix

murshid, ix, 107

music, 72, 135

mystic, 3, 45, 54, 121

mysticism, 13, 14, 47, 121

name, 1, 18, 33, 35, 71, 95, 100, 125

nature, 8, 15, 25, 78, 94. 95. 117, 133

neighbors, 146

Omar Khayyám, 54

occult, 44, 54

ocean, 33, 40

pain, 11, 13, 69, 71, 95, 104, 120

passion, 23, 46, 99

patience, 66

peace, 5, 77, 88

personality, 15, 84

philosophy, 13
physical plane, 70
piety, 17
plants, 39, 91
pleasure, 11, 22, 69, 85, 104, 151
poison, 63
poverty, 11, 56
power, 3, 8, 68, 69, 75, 82, 105, 107, 109, 110, 120, 128, 139
praise, 31, 37, 82, 129
prayer, 25, 30, 99, 123, 128, 137, 138
pride, 77
priest, 21, 25
prophet, 21
psychic, 44, 54
purpose, 72, 80, 88, 1116, 117, 118
race, 122
reason, 8, 9, 119, 121, 136
records, 52
reed, 135
reformer, 21
religion, 3, 6, 7, 13, 21, 37, 58, 63, 86, 121, 134
remedy, 120
renunciation, 20, 116
revelation, 1, 53, 78
reward, 56
riches, 56, 68, 82
riders, 27
rock, 13, 74
roses, 63, 144
sacrifice, 15, 115

INDEX

saqi, ix
science, 121
scripture, 117, 133
sea, 42, 43, 135, 143, 146, 151
secrets, 42, 43, 66, 119
self-pity, 11, 103
service, 71, 120
shadow, 2, 65, 84, 92, 111
shell, 10, 132
shrine, 7, 27
sin, 13, 30, 86, 142
sincerity, 10, 31, 40, 71, 72, 139
single-mindedness, 7
sleep, 45, 74, 85, 98
solitude, 144
songs, 52
sorrow, 66, 81, 103, 142
sovereign, 7, 24, 38, 68, 112
soul, 10, 11, 19, 21, 22, 26, 31, 35, 37, 39, 44, 46, 65. 67, 69, 70, 71, 73, 80, 84, 85, 90, 92, 96, 97, 99, 100, 105, 106, 115, 116, 117, 118, 119, 122, 129, 131, 134, 144, 152
space, 1
speech, 52, 132
spiritualism, 54
spirit, 37, 39, 53, 54, 59, 88, 89, 122, 146
spirituality, 17, 111
stream, 1, 42, 113
student, 32, 33, 110, 126
study, 15, 86
success, 9, 22, 43, 132, 148

Sun, 2, 26, 32, 39, 75
sympathy, ix, 37, 38, 83, 98
tailor, 88
tax, 100
teacher, 32, 33, 42, 86, 108, 110
teaching, 6, 54, 113, 126
thorns, 84, 144
thought, 6, 51, 53, 65, 68, 69, 98, 105, 123, 131, 132, 139
time, 1, 22
tolerance, 3, 20, 32, 61, 66, 106
torch, 70
treasure, 56, 93, 97, 101
trees, 5, 25, 106, 133, 147, 148
trouble, 11, 91
true self, 4, 44
truth, 1, 2, 3, 22, 28, 29, 32, 34, 40, 46, 49, 59, 63, 123, 124, 125, 128, 134, 143, 147
unity, 16, 45, 51, 119
understanding, 61, 78, 91, 93, 133
universe, 18, 75, 99
vanity, 111
veils, 2, 49, 55, 68, 69
vibration, 16, 18
vice, 105
victory, 30, 67
vigilance, 83
virtue, 5, 13, 30, 57, 86, 105, 118
vision, 30, 40, 67, 77, 89, 120
vocation, 73
water, 1, 87, 108, 113, 118, 127, 133, 146, 150

INDEX

waves, 42, 43, 135, 146, 151
weakness, 20, 108
wealth, 49
will, 5, 8, 9, 43, 107, 110, 142, 149
wine, ix, 54
wine-bearer, ix
wings, 100
wisdom, 15, 17, 18, 31, 55, 58, 68, 78, 79, 80, 81, 93, 97, 113, 117, 119, 133, 142, 144, 146, 149
wood, 4, 135
words, 10, 42, 65, 83, 93, 96, 97, 105, 126, 132, 133
worship, 40, 46, 95, 123

Hazrat Inayat Khan was born in Baroda, India, on July 5th, 1882. A master of Indian classical music, he gave up a brilliant career as a musician to devote himself full-time to the spiritual path. In 1910, he followed his master's direction to go to the West to "spread the wisdom of Sufism" in the United States, England, and throughout Europe. For a decade and a half, he traveled tirelessly, giving lectures and guiding an ever-growing group of Western spiritual seekers. In 1926, he returned to India and died there the following year, on February 5th, 1927. He is entombed in the precincts of the *dargah* of Hazrat Nizam ad-Din Awliya'. Today, the universalist Sufi teachings he spread continue to inspire countless people around the world, and his spiritual heirs may be found in every corner of the planet.

www.ingramcontent.com/pod-product-compliance
Lightning Source LLC
Chambersburg PA
CBHW052101280426
43673CB00071B/45